Be Good to Your Body
Learning Yoga

Roz Fulcher

Dover Publications, Inc.
Mineola, New York

Bibliographical Note

Be Good to Your Body—Learning Yoga is a new work, first published by Dover Publications, Inc., in 2013.

International Standard Book Number

ISBN-13: 978-0-486-48830-1
ISBN-10: 0-486-48830-6

Manufactured in the United States by Courier Corporation
48830601
www.doverpublications.com

Note

Many people around the world practice yoga, a set of exercises designed to help you become physically fit, as well as relaxed and stress-free. Yoga originated in India and has been practiced for around 5,000 years! There are many forms of yoga, but most are focused on improving breathing and physical strength. Many people also practice meditation, a mental "exercise" that helps to calm the mind. This book will teach you dozens of yoga "poses," describing exactly how to move and position your body. Follow the directions carefully, and soon you'll be doing poses such as the Crocodile, the Double-Sandwich, the Roaring Lion, and the Pretzel with confidence. For added fun, you can color in the pages, too.

IMPORTANT NOTE: Any exercise can cause injury to the body, including yoga. Before you start any of the yoga poses, tell an adult, who should be available to supervise. If any of the poses feels uncomfortable or is painful, STOP right away. Although yoga is pretty safe when done correctly, it's always possible that an injury can occur.

Backbends

Backbends are used to energize the body. They create strength and elasticity for your back and spine as well as the legs and shoulders.

At first, it may be difficult to grab your ankles but with practice it will become easy.

Camel Pose

Start in a tall kneeling position with the tops of your feet flat on the ground and your knees slightly apart. Reach around and take hold of each ankle with your hands, arching your back and lifting your chest to make the shape of a "camel's hump." If comfortable, let your head fall back. Hold the stretch for a few seconds. Then support your lower back with your hands and slowly come back into an upright position.

Rocking Horse

Lie on your belly. Bend your knees and reach back for your ankles with your hands. Squeeze and lift both thighs and shoulders, raising your feet and chest as much as possible. Take strong breaths in and out as you begin to rock back and forth. Rest in the "child's pose" (pg. 12) when you get tired.

Yoga Breathing

One of the major principles of yoga is controlled breathing, called "Pranayama." This type of breathing helps one focus on the moment while calming and grounding the mind.

Here are some fun examples of controlled breathing:

hummmmm

Bumble Bee Breath

Sit comfortably with your spine tall and straight. Close your eyes and take a slow deep breath in through your nose. Imitating a bee, exhale "hummmm" as long as possible. Repeat several times.

Elevator Breathing

Imagine your breath is an elevator taking a ride through your body. Inhale and start the elevator ride to the "top floor," your head. Breathe out and feel your elevator breath take all your troubles and worries down through your chest, belly, legs, and out through the elevator doors in your feet.

5, 4, 3, 2, 1

Take 5

Sit comfortably. While breathing through your nose, count in your mind "1, 2, 3, 4, 5." Pause. As you exhale count backwards in your mind "5, 4, 3, 2, 1." Repeat several times as you feel your body relax.

What is Yoga?

The word yoga, loosely translated, means "union" because yoga involves a combination of breathing and mental relaxation.

Yoga is a form of exercise that is about 5,000 years ago, originating in India.

6

Sunrise-Sunset

The sunrise-sunset pose is a good all-over warm-up exercise.

As you inhale, think of the rising sun; as you exhale and fold, think of the setting sun.

In yoga, movement and breathing work together. For example, you stretch on the inhale and relax on the exhale.

Stand up tall and take 3 to 5 breaths. On the next inhale, lift your arms above your head. As you exhale, bend the upper half of your body toward your waist down toward your legs as if you are diving into a pool. Bend as far as you comfortably can. As you inhale again, open your arms wide and stand up slowly, stretching your arms to the sky again. Repeat several times.

The Candlestick

This pose is also known as the shoulder stand.

The "candlestick" stretches the spine, helping it to stay long and strong.

This position increases blood flow to the brain and also helps headaches, congestion, and sore throats.

Lie flat on the floor with your arms along the sides of your body with your palms facing down. Bend your knees into your chest while exhaling, then lift them up, pointing your toes to the ceiling. Bend your elbows and place your hands flat on your back while holding this pose to keep your balance. Concentrate on your breathing and stay in this pose for several breaths. Slowly bring your legs back down to your chest and then to the floor.

Cat-Cow Pose

The cat and cow poses are often paired to create a nice flow that uses breath to create movement in the spine.

These poses stretch the back, torso, and neck, providing massage to the spine and internal organs.

Cat pose arches the back, similar to a cat when it is stretching.

* Kneel on all fours with back straight, hands below the shoulders, and knees below the hips.

* Inhale, look up to the ceiling allowing your back to arch. (cow pose) Exhale and arch your back in opposite position, head facing down. (cat pose)

* Repeat, inhaling as you look down and exhaling as you look up, stretching as much as possible in both directions.

Moooo!

Cow pose imitates the sway back of a cow.

11

Child's Pose

The child's pose imitates the positioning of a baby in the mother's womb. This is a "static" pose, which means it is a pose that is held without moving the body for a few seconds.

This pose relaxes the mind and relieves tension in the back.

This pose is a good way to begin or end a stretching session. Kneel with your feet touching and knees slightly apart. Slowly bend over and touch your forehead to the floor. Your arms can be at the sides, palms facing up or in front of your head with palms on the floor. Inhale and exhale slowly and deeply. Hold child's pose for 3 to 5 breaths.

Cobra

Cobras are venomous snakes that use their strong spines to slither across the ground and even climb trees.

This pose strengthens the spine and stretches your lungs, shoulders, and abdomen.

Lie on your belly, placing your hands under your shoulders. Press yourself up, arching your back. Lift your chest until your arms are almost straight. Try not to place too much weight on your hands but use your strong back muscles to lift as high as possible. Look up to the ceiling. Hold briefly and hiss like a snake; then slowly come back down.

Dancer Pose

Stand with feet apart. Bending your right knee, grasp the inside of your right foot with your right hand. Raise your left hand overhead as you lift your right foot behind and up. Allow your torso to move forward, opening the chest. Balance on one foot for a few breaths. Repeat on the opposite side.

This pose develops both physical and mental concentration. It tones and lengthens the leg and hip muscles while improving your balancing skills.

Partner Variation

Stand facing your partner a few feet apart, being careful not to butt heads.
Have each partner raise left arm to touch the others above the head.
Grasp the inside of the right foot behind you. Smile at one another and keep
your balance.

Crocodile

Crocodiles are active hunters but also relaxed creatures that enjoy basking in the sun.

This practice strengthens the arms and wrists and is also a great core workout.

Kneel on all fours; then straighten your legs into plank (flat) position. Slowly lower your body, keeping your elbows in, touching your ribs. Hold your body slightly off the ground for the "hunting" crocodile position. Relax to the floor with your head to the side for the "relaxing" crocodile. Practice this pose 2 or 3 times in a row.

16

The Dolphin

The dolphin pose is very similar to downard dog but avoids stress on the wrists.

This pose strengthens the arms and legs while stretching the shoulders, hamstrings, calves, and arches.

Start on your knees and arms. Clasp your hands together and push up on your toes. Press yourself up on your legs and walk your feet toward your elbows. Keep your elbows on the ground with your head down. Stay in this position for 5-6 breaths and slowly release back to the ground.

17

The Double Boat

Sit opposite your partner, about 3 feet between you. Hold your hands on the outside of your legs. Raise both legs and place the soles of your feet together. Work on finding your balance, and when you are ready, try straightening your legs. Stay here for 5 breaths and then slowly lower your legs down to the ground and release your hands.

The Double-Sandwich

Sit opposite your partner with the soles of your feet together. Fold forward and if you can, reach for each other's hands. Try and tuck your chin in and relax your chest down to your thighs. Hold for a few breaths and then release. Make sure neither of you is feeling pain or discomfort—this is supposed to feel good.

If you can't reach each other's hands, have each person grab the end of a hand towel.

As long as you are feeling the stretch in your lower back and hamstrings, you are doing it right.

Downward Dog

Begin on your hands and knees. Your wrists should be underneath your shoulders and your knees underneath your hips. Lift your hips, moving into the shape of an upside down "v." Work on straightening your legs and lowering your heels to the ground. Relax your head between your arms and direct your gaze through your legs or up toward your belly button. Hold for 5 breaths.

This pose strengthens your hands, wrists, and lower back and is a great way to stretch your calves.

Downward dog is the most basic and widely known yoga pose.

The Flamingo

The Flamingo posture is like the "tree pose" but easier to hold.

Flamingos stand on one leg using 3 long forward-pointing toes and a hind toe to help them balance.

Stand up tall and tuck your hands under your shoulders to make your wings. Bend on one knee and lift it up off the ground. Balance for 5 breaths, release, and balance on the opposite leg.

The Dragon

Try doing these poses to build strength by timing each other with a stopwatch to see how long you can stay in your pose.

roarrrrr...

Get on your hands and knees. Step one foot back into a lunge. Place your front knee directly over your ankle and your back knee on the mat. Place your hands on your front thigh. Take in a deep breath like a dragon. Inhale deeply through your nose and reach your arms up, placing your palms together above your head. Stick out your tongue and roar like a dragon.

Baby Dragon

Twisted Dragon

23

Freeze Tag Yoga

Game

Gather a group of players and choose one to be "it." The player that is "it" will chase the others, trying to catch and tag them. Once a player has been tagged, he or she must "freeze" into a yoga pose. Continue until everyone is frozen. The last player tagged takes over as "it."

Variation - Players can "save" other players that are frozen by tagging them as they run by.

Gorilla Pose

This pose is excellent for releasing tight hamstrings that can cause back pain.

While doing this pose, imagine you are like the gorilla with its strong and calm presence.

For extra "oomph," tuck your hands under your toes.

Start with feet a few inches apart. Bend your knees deeply and let your body fall forward, bringing your chest to your thighs. Let your arms and head hang heavily. Now, begin to straighten your legs, drawing your tailbone to the ceiling. Keep your chest close to your thighs and stay in this position for 3 breaths.

Legs-Up-a-Wall

This pose is known to "cure whatever ails you." Besides that, this pose stretches your calves, hamstrings, back, and neck.

This is a great pose to do after a long day on your feet.

Place a yoga mat or blanket on the floor next to a wall. Lie on your side close to the wall with your legs to one side. Roll onto your back as you place your legs up the wall. Add a bolster or cushion under your hips if it feels more comfortable. Relax your hands out to your sides, face up. Stay in this position for at least 5 minutes and focus on slow deep breaths.

Lying Twist

The lying twist is another pose which is very simple yet extremely effective. It soothes the spine, warms the neck, and frees your lower back/hips.

Doing this pose will increase strength and muscle tone in your midsection.

Lie on your back with your knees bent. Inhale and hug your knees to your chest. Exhale and stretch your arms out to your sides. Lower your legs to the right and turn your head to the left to deepen the stretch.

Roaring Lion

Start in a kneeling position with knees shoulder-width apart. Spread your knees comfortably with calves flat on the floor. Place both hands on your knees and "splay" your fingers like lion's claws. Keep shoulders back and avoid slouching.

Lift your chest up just enough to straighten your back.

This is among the best face exercises, benefiting the jaw, throat, mouth, and tongue.

Take a deep breath through your nose. At the same time, lower your jaw and open your mouth as wide as possible. Stretch your tongue out and curl it down as far as you can towards your chin. Roll your eyes upwards and fix your gaze between your eyebrows. Spread your splayed fingers further and then exhale. Perform this three times, with a rest in between each.

Lotus Pose

This is a yoga classic and is one of the most recognized poses.

The lotus is a relaxing pose that will help you calm down after a hectic day. Stay in this position for a few deep breaths.

Sit on the floor and bend your right knee, grasping the right foot with both hands and placing it on top of the left thigh, bringing the heel as close to the belly button as possible. Repeat with the the left leg, placing it up on the right thigh. Keep your spine straight but not rigid.

Monkey Pose

The monkey pose is most commonly known as the "split."

Start from a kneeling position. Inhale and extend your right leg forward with your heel touching the floor. Lean forward slightly and place the palms of your hands on the floor on either side of your outstretched leg. Exhale and slowly slide your right leg forward and your left leg straight back until you reach a full split. If you are comfortable, lift both arms over your head and reach up. Hold for 3 breaths and repeat with your other leg.

Mountain Pose

When standing in the mountain pose, the mind is quiet and the body is strong and still like a mountain.

Mountain pose is the foundation of many yoga poses.

Mountain pose promotes good posture and helps focus your mind.

Stand upright with your feet together. Tense your thigh muscles so that your legs feel solid like a rock. Lift your chest and stand tall with your shoulders relaxed. Keep your arms down to your sides with your body in a straight line from head to toe.

Namaste

"Namaste" is a common practice in yoga and is generally used at the beginning and end of a class or session. It is a gesture of respect from one to another or even for yourself. To perform Namaste, place your hands together and bring them to the front of your face. As you bow your head bring your hands down to the middle of your chest/heart and close your eyes.

Musical Mats

Game:

Set out one yoga mat per player in a circle on the floor. Have players write their favorite yoga pose on an index card and place one on each yoga mat. Choose fun and upbeat music to stop and start during the game. Before playing, review with everyone, making sure that they are familiar with the yoga poses chosen.

36

Have players stand in a circle outside of the mats. When the music starts, players can then start hopping and skipping around the mats. When music stops, players step on the mat in front of them and perform the pose listed on the card. Hold for a few breaths, release, and turn music back on. Repeat.

The Plank

The Plank pose is an excellent arm and core strengthener.

If you are building strength and stamina, hold for as long as possible.

Begin on your hands and knees with your wrists directly under your shoulders. Tuck your toes and step back with your feet bringing your head and your body into one straight line. Keep your thighs lifted and don't let your hips sink too low. Hold for 5 breaths. Release and move into "child's pose" to rest your muscles.

The Pretzel

The pretzel is a twisting pose. The twisting action helps your back muscles relax and when the twist is released the areas involved flood with fresh blood and nutrients.

Sit on the ground. Shift to the right and lift your right leg over your left one, placing the foot against the outside of the left knee. Keep your spine straight. Stretch your arms out to the sides and twist around to the right. Now bring your left arm down on the outside of your right knee and hold your right foot with your left hand. Place your right hand on the floor behind you. Exhale and twist as far as possible to the right, looking over your right shoulder. Release and repeat on the other side.

The Ragdoll

To do a ragdoll pose, stand comfortably and reach arms up high. Bend knees slightly as you bend forward. Let your head hang down along with your arms (or you can hold arms together). Relax your muscles and "let go." Shake your head "yes," shake your head "no." Take in deep breaths and feel your body sink further into the floor with every exhale. To finish, slowly roll yourself back to standing.

This is a great pose for opening the hips and lowering blood pressure.

Sit in a chair comfortably with your feet and knees a hip distance apart. Make sure your knees are over your ankles and that your feet are facing forward. Reach up on your inhale and then bring your torso down and over your knees on the exhale. Bring your hands to the floor and let your head hang down. Inhale and exhale slowly, releasing your tension with each breath.

Puppy Pose

Start on your hands and knees with your shoulders directly above your wrists, and hips in line with your knees. Exhale and move your hips backwards about half way to your heels. Drop your forehead down and feel the stretch in your arms. Stay in this relaxed position for 30 seconds to 1 minute, then rest your buttocks onto your knees and release.

Seesaw

Grab a partner and sit on the floor facing each other with your legs split in a "v." Reach out and clasp each other's hands. As one partner leans forward, the other leans back, pulling each other into the bend slowly. "Seesaw" back and forth, making sure to stretch only as far as is comfortable.

43

Star Pose

This pose energizes the body and provides a good stretch for the legs, shoulders, arms. It also opens the chest, which allows for deeper breathing.

Balance on one leg to make the pose more challenging. Remember to breathe.

Stand tall and spread your feet wide apart. Raise your arms and reach out as if someone is pulling your arms out with a piece of string. Press your feet into the ground and take a deep breath in. Slowly release breath. Repeat 3 times.

Butterfly Pose

This pose stretches the inner thighs and hips and is great to do after running.

This stretch also removes tiredness from long hours of standing and walking.

Sit on the floor and bend your knees, bringing the soles of your feet together. Sit with your spine straight and take in a deep breath. Exhale and press your thighs and knees downward. Now, relax your breathing and like the wings of a butterfly flap both knees up and down. Start slowly and then increase the speed slightly. Flap, flap, flap!

Table and Chair

The table pose is the starting point for many floor postures and helps lengthen and realign the spine.

Sit on the floor with your legs straight in front of you. Inhale and place the palms of your hands just behind your hips. Bend your knees and lift your hips until your torso and hips make a straight line. Hold briefly, then release the pose back down.

Stand upright on your mat in "mountain pose." Inhale and place your feet hip-width apart. Stretch your arms out in front of you at shoulder height, keeping your fingers together. Exhale and bend down as if you were about to sit in a chair. Hold briefly and then stand upright again.

This pose strengthens the lower body while stretching the upper back.

Tree Pose

Imagine your toes are the roots grounded in the earth. Your standing leg is the trunk, strong and tall. Your arms and bent leg are branches reaching outward and upward toward the sun.

This pose strengthens your thighs, calves, ankle, and spine and develops mental stability.

Stand tall, feet together. Find something in front of you to focus on. Extend your arms out to the side and lift your right foot. Bend your knee, placing your right foot above or below the left knee. To test your balance, bring your hands in to a prayer position in front of your heart or raise above your head.

Triple Hills

This pose gets its name from the two humps your bottom makes and the tall hill your joined arms make.

This is a great total body stretch. With a partner you get a more intense stretch in the upper back, shoulders and hamstrings.

Stand facing your partner about a foot apart. Press your hands together, palm to palm, and step away from each other. Lean forward and push your hands up above your heads as high as you can. Stare into each other's eyes or tuck your chin down to your chest. Arch your spine for a deeper stretch. Breathe steadily for 5-6 breaths and then release slowly.

Turtle Pose

Turtle pose is an intense forward bend which helps calm the mind, reduce stress, and stretch the groin.

Sit with legs bent but wide apart. Work your torso between your knees, wrapping your arms under your legs and grasping your ankles, or laying them out, palms flat on the floor. Try to straighten your legs and lower your torso to the ground, resting your chin on the floor.

The Windmill

Start by standing with your feet forward and a little wider than shoulder-width apart. Spread your arms out to the sides making a "t." Bend forward from the waist and reach down with your right hand to touch your left foot, with your left hand stretched to the ceiling. Hold for a few breaths and then switch sides, bringing your left hand to touch your right foot now, with your right arm reached to the ceiling. Repeat a few times.

The Warrior

The warrior poses take strength, steadiness, and a fierce determination to hold them.

Warrior Pose I : The front knee is bent, back leg straight, arms extended overhead, and the chest turned in the same direction as the bent knee.

These poses are named after the great hero warrior Virabhadra from Hindu mythology. He was described as having a thousand feet, a thousand eyes, and as fighting with a thousand clubs.

Warrior Pose II : The front knee is bent, back leg straight, arms extended out to the sides in line with the legs.

Warrior Pose III: Balancing on one straight leg with the trunk and arms extending horizontally forward and the lifted leg extended back.

53

Boat Pose

The boat pose is a powerful core workout. By strengthening your core you will have better posture and be able to run and jump with more strength and coordination.

If this is too difficult at first, hold onto your knees until you get stronger. Keep practicing.

Sit, feet stretched on the ground. Lean back and put your arms behind your back with your toes pointed. Lift up your legs, using your stomach muscles to control your legs as they lift. Try to stretch your arms out in front of you. Hold the pose as long as possible. When you think you can't hold it any longer, hold for 2 more breaths and then release.

The Bridge

This is a backbend pose that strengthens the spine, opens the chest, improves spinal flexibility, and stimulates the thyroid.

Lie on your back. Bend your knees and lift your hips up towards the ceiling. Straighten your arms, pressing them down into the mat. Roll one shoulder and then the other. Lift the hips higher, drawing your chest towards the chin. Take a couple of breaths, then release the hands and bring your back down.

Yoga Ball

The yoga stability ball is a fun way to get extra support for moves that require endurance and flexibility. It also adds a balance challenge to some poses.

Seated Stork Pose

Sit on the ball and cross your left foot over your right knee. Bring the palms together in front of your chest. Inhale and take your arms overhead. Hold for 3 breaths. Lower and repeat on the other side.

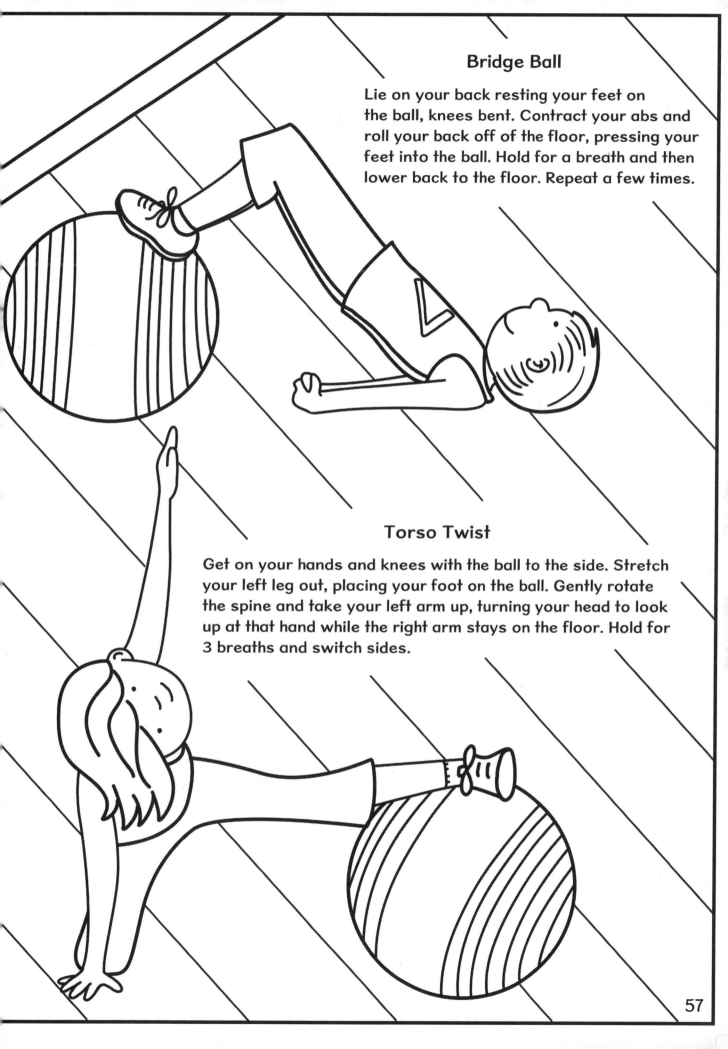

Bridge Ball

Lie on your back resting your feet on the ball, knees bent. Contract your abs and roll your back off of the floor, pressing your feet into the ball. Hold for a breath and then lower back to the floor. Repeat a few times.

Torso Twist

Get on your hands and knees with the ball to the side. Stretch your left leg out, placing your foot on the ball. Gently rotate the spine and take your left arm up, turning your head to look up at that hand while the right arm stays on the floor. Hold for 3 breaths and switch sides.

During a long day of sitting, your body will appreciate some yoga postures to energize and reduce muscle tension.

Before returning to your work give yourself a few minutes to relax. Simply cross your arms and rest your head.

Sit in your chair and cross your right leg over your left knee. Flex both feet and lift them off of the floor. "Thread the needle" by clasping your hands around your left leg, just under the knee.

"Yogi Says"

"Yogi says do the tree pose."

Game:

Choose a leader and play this game as you would "Simon Says." The leader performs a pose, and if he says, "Yogi Says," players must also perform the pose. If the leader performs the pose without first saying, "Yogi says," the player who performs the pose is "out." Continue until you have one remaining player, who becomes the winner and takes over as the "Yogi."

Corpse Pose

Lie down on your back and place your hands by your hips facing upward. Spread your feet a bit wider than hips-distance apart. Close your eyes, relax, and breathe deeply and evenly. Relax your body for 5 to 10 minutes if possible.

Trying to lie still and not "think" is challenging. As thoughts come into your mind, try to put them aside until later and focus on your breathing instead.

This pose relaxes the mind and relieves headaches, fatigue, and insomnia.